I0571091

For This Cause
Writers Unite

A *SteamyT Pub*
Young Writers Flow Project
Steamy Trails Publishing

For This Cause
Writers Unite

ISBN-13: 978-0-9851185-0-1
ISBN-10: 0985118504

Company: Steamy Trails Publishing
Trademark: SteamyT Pub
Logo Design by T. Andrew Campbell

Printed in the USA

Dedication

This project is dedicated to young writers with a dream of becoming published authors. Steamy Trails Publishing wants to encourage our youth to be all they can be one page at a time.

For more information visit:

www.steamytrailspublishing.com

Promoting Literacy

Acknowledgements

The completion of this book has been a direct labor of love and we appreciate all the people involved with making this first edition possible and through your hard work, dedication and raw talent Steamy Trails Publishing has put together an amazing collaboration of wonderful work to display.

We are proud to have with us (writers are listed in order of submission entry) are The beautiful Sharon Smith, The multi-faceted Tiffany Christina Lewis, The incomparable Nike Binger Marshall, Publisher Katrina Gurl, The reigning Queen Gloria J. Lathan, The powerful Emmanuel Brown, The newcomer Evangeline, The passionate poet Kewayne Andre Clark Wadley, The ever sensual Robert Moore, The multitalented Fiordaliza Charles, The soulful poet Eddie Lamar Sharpe Jr., The Incredible Damon K. Kimbrough, The greatest G. D. Grace, The writer of courage Michael Charles Givens and last but not least, WiL Palazzo, the writer with supernatural talent.

These amazing array of people lined up in this book are nothing less than a rainbow of beauty that will shine on every page turned.

Table of Contents

(In entry submission order)

Foreword

It is with great pleasure and honor, as part of the SteamyT Pub team, that I write this foreword. SteamyT Pub has put together a great group of awesome writers and poets, who have come together for a beautiful cause; to help young writers shine.

There are so many young talented writers with the gift and skill to tell a story, through poetry, shorts, and even novels that we want to find ways that will encourage them to keep writing and share their visions of the mind with the world. The SteamyT Pub team is committed to this project that will help continue the literary movement for our youth. We could think of no better way to get a jump start with this project then to recruit other talented writers who believe in our youth and who are more than willing to share their gift of writing for this anthology.

Reading the work of these awesome writers will give you a feeling of emotion, not only because you know that their participation in this project is part of an effort to help a young writer, but also because they are sharing their own gift with you to read and feel.

I'm sure you will enjoy this anthology of writings as much as I have. This is just the beginning of this project and many more publications for this project will follow.

Congratulations to the participants and the readers of this work, for supporting our effort to continue to help "*Young Writers Flow*".

~Nita Bee~

SteamyT Pub Team (Detroit)

www.steamytrailspublishing.com

Nita Bee's Buzzin' WebBlog

www.nitabee.com

Introduction

"I WAS HERE" is a common quote that can be heard, understood and accepted by all humans; no matter the race, color, creed or background. We all want to have the certain knowledge that we have made a difference as we've walk through this thing we call life.

The sole purpose of "SteamyT Pub Anthology Books" is to serve and up build the future of our youth by helping them to have a voice through their own published work. If we encourage our youth to use their gifts and talents in writing, we also encourage them to have a positive voice in our society. Therefore, we also help them to secure a positive future that will benefit us all. Steamy Trails Publishing is dedicated to the success of our youth!

"We are what we think we are, we become what we believe we can and we achieve our greatest dreams through the encouragement of our peers" ~ Katrina Gurl

Warning: Some content may contain mature language

For This Cause Writers Unite

For This Cause Writers Unite:

A SteamyT Pub
Young Writers Flow Project

For This Cause Writers Unite

STEPPING STONES
by Sharon Smith

the first
Phyllis Wheatley
humanity hymn

love is
Yolanda Cornelia "Nikki Giovanni"
talking black

personal letter
Wilsonia "Sonia" Benita Sanchez
morning haiku's

singing sin
Gwendolyn Brooks
real cool

expecting nothing
Alice Walker
* said to poetry*

caged bird
 Maya Angelou
phenomenally still rising

Empty (formally known as WOE)
by Sharon Smith

On my walk this morning
my eyes cried emotionless tears
that I wish my brain knew
to save for this moment.
With my heart in your pocket
you walked out
leaving me
hollow
and
 I have
not
 a tear
to cry.

BE U TO THE FULLEST
by Sharon Smith

Looking before me
straight ahead,
I see the most beautiful creature.

I say:
Every morning when I wake
it's for you.
Your happiness is my strength.
My love or you is never ending.
Even in death I will love you.
Who is to say that I won't?
All that I am
and all that I hope to be
it's all in me
through you.
Your loyalty is irreplaceable
and I'm grateful to have you
on my team.
No one will ever understand
this powerful love,
the power of this love.
Some say it's ridiculous
I say it's mine, all mine,
and no one can ever interrupt it.
Each step,
each breath,
each smile,
yours.
Every part of you is me,
and I am you.
I love me some you,
through and through,
because you are
so beautiful.

Be You To the Fullest today!
Then I turn from the mirror
to start my day.

Haiku's
by Sharon Smith

Watching you closely
your sexy lips and tongue tricks
I need you like air

To kiss Guillermo
What makes him tick I wonder
Sexy male poet

I'm not plowing fields
You will forever be mine
Don't you forget that

Making decisions
About life's joys and sorrows
The sky is so clear

I am spring cleaning
Out with you and your bull crap
Spring cleaning now done

Personal Letter #1
by Sharon Smith

and so I guess
this is the end
I told myself
You were my friend
And then I said
I would not cry
yet here we are
crushed, crumbled, shattered
and my eyes told
the whole story
of my broken heart

LOVE COLLAGE
by Sharon Smith

Love doesn't make the world go round,
It just makes it a fascinating ride.
I feel lucky every day to have you.
So,
tell me how I am your number one choice
and let me have my way, always
because
after you fall in love
your life will be forever changed
and no matter how hard you try,
that feeling for that love, will never dissipate
because
love is a fruit that's always in season,
we love simply because we cannot help it.
So,
Love me daily, and love me deep
because
my heart belongs to you.

Steamy Trails publishing personally appreciates
Sharon Smith for donating her time and talent to this
cause. To find out about more about Sharon and of
her work visit:
www.facebook.com/sgrantsmith

How has the "Steamy Trails" entity helped your literary
goals?

"The encouragement is priceless" ~ Sharon Smith

Karma
by Tiffany Christina Lewis

Dolphins sleep with their eyes open. Just like cheaters. I know this, because I am one. Not a dolphin, a cheater. I was the girl rounding out a night of passionate sex with tip toeing into the house and sneaking in bed. My boyfriend usually woke up ranting. I'd sell him some line about being too drunk to drive or losing track of time. He usually bought it.

That's why I could never be married. I'm a free spirit. I really shouldn't even have a boyfriend but Travis keeps a roof over my head. He supplies my addictions: partying, sex and nonstop fun. Sometimes, I enjoy those things with him but usually I get those things without him. I use his money to make my life more comfortable.

Do I feel guilty? Not at all. I make sure I use protection when I fool around. I've even told some of my guys about my boyfriend. They feel victorious because they get to be with me while he waits at home, but they don't know that they are temporary. He could never be replaced. I know it all sounds kinda warped but, it works for me.

One hot July night I got the itch and I needed Bryce to scratch it. Bryce Jones. He had a long finger and his scratching was the best. I texted him and without hesitation he told me to come on over. I called my friend Nicole and conspicuously made some plans to go to her house for drinks. She was always good for an alibi. I grabbed my coat and was out the door before Travis's kiss could dry on my cheek.

When I arrived at Bryce's house I knocked on the door for what felt like 10 minutes. Finally I banged on the door as loud as I could and shouted for Bryce to open up. The door swung open and I was warmly greeted by his wife, who I didn't know existed. She must have been part feline because when she opened that door, and without even one word, the claws came out. I was caught off guard and easily defeated. I made my escape in the elevator, bruised and bleeding. When I got back to my car I called Nicole to tell her that I really would be coming for those drinks but she didn't answer.

I sulked home. My itch had been scratched all right, by Bryce's wife, so I guess I could go home and cuddle with Travis. He would believe my story about someone on the street trying to mug me and that I fought them off bravely. He would hold me lovingly and dress my wounds. He would tell me he loves me and I would say "You too." I would fall asleep before we could make love and wake up before him, well rested and bright eyed.

I walked into the house and it was dark. All the lights were off and I could hear a faint noise. TV? No. I walked slowly towards the bedroom. Radio? No. By the time my hand touched the doorknob I knew what I was hearing. It was an unmistakable sound. I had made it out of my own mouth more than enough times to know what it was. I even made other people make that sound, very often.

I swung open the door and my eyes could not believe what I was seeing.
My boyfriend and my best friend.
Travis and Nicole.
Making love.

Carefree and happy.
Genuinely happy to be together.

They stopped and looked at me; half surprised, half arrogant. Nicole looked radiant. Sweat touched her skin gently and her hair matted neatly to her forehead. Travis lay on top of her. His muscles were taught in a way I had never seen. He was actually sexy. After the 2 seconds it took me to take in the scene, my mind opened up again. For once I was seeing something real, something that I couldn't control. I was suddenly enraged.

"What the fuck is this?!" I shouted.

Karma.

Thrill of the Chase
by Tiffany Christina Lewis

The idea of murder is so blah. It's the action I crave. Pulse pounding chases in the woods to meet the end against an oak tree, or to narrowly escape death, leaning to the left of the knife. You go dashing through the brush like a frightened doe, feeling like your feet are stuck to the ground, when you are actually moving faster than lightning strikes. Breaking from the forest, bright lights appear up ahead. Is it your savior or an angel of death? This is when you pass out. Where will you wake?

Not As Planned
by Tiffany Christina Lewis

"Tell us what happened Ms. Lebec."

She sighed deeply. "I have made numerous statements about that night,"

"I understand that Ms. Lebec but we need you to tell us again, what happened the night of January 13th."

Loretta Lebec shivered; just hearing that date was enough to make her sweat nervously.

"Ms. Lebec, please tell us what happened that night. The jury is waiting."

Loretta took a deep breath and began to speak clearly and cautiously, as she had many times before, about her experience. "Nate showed up to my place at 8 that night,"

"Mr. Nate Parker? Our comatose and unavailable witness?"

"Yes, he showed up at 8 pm. I had prepared us dinner, grilled chicken, stir fried vegetables and mashed potatoes, his favorite," she wiped her tears. "We ate dinner and sat down to watch a movie. At around 10:30 there was a knock on the door. It was King."

"King? Mr. Leon Parker? The deceased?"

"Yes," she paused, "King, he had a scary look on his face."

"Can you elaborate?"

"His lips were curled up in a snarl, his eyes were wide as saucers, and he looked deranged. He had his hands on the door frame, leaning into the apartment. He said 'Where is Nate?'"

"Ms. Lebec, how are all of you related in this situation?"

Loretta sighed, her dirty secret was now on trial, "King and Nate are twin brothers. I was King's girlfriend and I was seeing Nate."

"Did Leon know you were seeing his twin brother?"

"At this point, I assume so," she scoffed.

"So before he showed up that night, you assumed he did not know." The prosecutor said with a slight attitude. His patience was short for Loretta.

"Yes."

"Okay, please continue."

Loretta wrung her hands, "I told King that Nate wasn't there. That's when King said he wanted to come in. I was at a loss for words, so I stood there, probably looking stupid. King pushed past me. I stumbled and after getting my balance I ran over to try and stop him. I grabbed his arm and he turned around and slapped me." she stopped breathing for a moment, tears began to wash her face. "I heard King laughing when he reached the living room,

"Long nights brother?" King Smiled.

"King," Nate was standing with his hands in his pockets.

"No excuses, Caliph," King called Nate by his nickname, "This is betrayal. Plain and fucking simple."

"I was going to tell you man,"

King laughed hysterically, "What, was this the first date?" he didn't wait for an answer, "NO! It's not! You don't tell someone that you're fucking his woman, AFTER you start doing it, that's just rude." his smiled faded. "Y'all already broke my trust, so," he reached behind his back and under his shirt. "Caliph, you already know the penalty for betrayal," King revealed a .45 caliber pistol. He pointed it at Caliph's chest.

"No King," Loretta said as she stood next to the television. She was next to King, not close enough to touch him, but if he had looked at her, he would be close enough to see the sweat bead run down her face. Loretta's living room had just become a very dangerous place.

Caliph stepped towards the couch, his hand reached out to his brother, pleading, "King, this is a little much," he cocked his head to the side.

"Haven't the streets taught you anything? Oh, I forgot, you left us for college! Shit ain't changed. Betrayal of this kind means death. Doesn't matter who you are and blood is not always thicker than water. Obviously!"

"King, please!" Loretta begged.

"Shut up you slut bitch! I smelled my brother on you weeks ago," he said, keeping his eyes on Caliph.

"No woman is worth dying for man," Caliph continued, "or going to jail for?"

"I'm not gonna get caught," King laughed menacingly.

Just then Loretta lunged forward onto King. The gun fired. Loretta screamed as they hit the floor. King's body was shaking with rage. He pushed Loretta off of him and stood up. Caliph was gone and so was King's gun.

"Bitch," he said with a laugh. He kicked her in the stomach. "Caliph! Where are you?!" King headed out of the living room and down the hall. Before he could reach the end of the hall Caliph sprung out of a room and grabbed him. They spun and twisted back into the room as they fought, almost synchronized. When one threw a punch, so did the other, when one tried to strangle one, the other did the same. They moved around the room with a furious grace until King finally got the better of Caliph.

Loretta entered the room. Caliph was in the air and being pushed through the second story window. The glass shattered and hit the floor, sounding like crystal rains. Loretta stood, dazed and in shock. They could hear Caliph's body hit the ground. King turned to her. "I hope you can fly, bitch." He said as he walked towards her.
She lifted her arms quickly.

"That's when I shot him."
"How many times did you shoot Leon Parker."
"Three."
"Twice in the chest and once in the leg, he died from a bullet in his heart. Don't you think that was a little excessive?"
"I was scared for my life,"
"Would you say this was an accident?"
"No, I would say it was self-defense."
"So you are admitting that you shot Leon Parker, three times, intentionally."
"I was in fear for my life! I was in fear that he was going to THROW ME out the damn window."
"Once was enough, I think." The prosecutor looked to the jury. "He would have been alive, and unable to throw you."
"Well, fear makes you react in ways that you may not think are logical."
"Ms. Lebec, what did you do after you shot Leon?"
"Dropped the gun. I stood in shock for a while then I ran over to the window to look for Nate. Once I saw him down there I ran out to go attend to him."
"So did you check on the victim at all, to see if he was okay?"
"I just said I looked out the window,"

The prosecutor smiled, "I'm sorry Ms. Lebec, Leon, is the victim here."

"I don't know about that," Loretta scoffed.

"Ms. Lebec, you are on trial for the murder of Leon Parker, he's the only one dead."

"Yea, he's dead because he assaulted me and Nate,"

The prosecutor interrupted, "No further questions."

In the case of the state versus Loretta Lebec for the murder of Leon Parker, the jury finds Ms. Lebec not guilty of first degree murder.

A week after her trial, Loretta arrived at St. Mary's hospital to visit Nate. He had come out of his coma just days before her arrival. She slipped into the room as the nurse checked Nate's vitals. Loretta leaned against the door frame. When they finally noticed her Nate smiled slyly.

"Hey Loretta."

"Hey Nate."

They greeted each other in the nonchalant way they had been forced to greet each other for years. They still felt like they were a secret even though they were more public than ever before. The nurse exited. Loretta slowly walked over and sat in the chair next to Nate's bed.

"Can I get a kiss woman?!" Nate said dramatically. "I been sleep for 4 months, you need to remind me of what life is like!"

She laughed, leaning over and kissing him. She surrendered her tongue to his waiting mouth. She had missed his kisses. They pulled apart from one another and Nate held her face gently. They looked lovingly at one another. He released her and Loretta sat next to him in a big comfy chair. This chair was for people who were waiting and waiting for a loved one to wake up. The hospital wanted them to be comfortable.

"So," he said after some waiting, "how was trial?"

"Couldn't be better than not guilty."

"Good. First degree murder was just not going to stick. How could they prove it was premeditated?"

Loretta didn't answer that question, even though she could have. They sat quietly. Loretta held his hand, IV inserted. "I'm glad you stayed under so long."

"Oh,"

"Yea, I demanded my right to a speedy trial so they were forced to go on without you."

"What, you thought I'd screw up the story?"

"No." she smiled and put her forehead on Nate's bed, she was exhausted. "I told them he kicked me."

Nate laughed and then laughed again. "What a little liar." He laughed yet again. He stopped laughing just long enough to dry his tears. "That didn't really go as we planned, now did it?" he squeezed her hand.

Loretta looked up at him. Her brow was furrowed in confusion. She bit her lip and finally she said, "No. I guess it didn't."

Breaking Hearts
by Tiffany Christina Lewis

I'm sorry.
I can't be with you like this.
I am no longer aloof,
captivated by your kiss.

There is nothing good about you!
Not even the sex!
I'm sure I can do better
when I move on to the next.

I've given this talk,
time and time before,
packed my stuff
and headed out the door.

Not cause I was out of love,
or because I disliked this man.
It's all because I can't commit,
and he just won't understand.

As soon as I feel the pinch,
commitment rearing its ugly head,
I pull the plug on his hearts life support,
and I'm leaving him for dead.

I do not wish to be your woman,
on your arm at every event.
There is no perk that I can fathom,
that would make me stay and sit.

I do not think the day will come,
I'm not going to change my mind,
I will not stay here and be all yours,
breaking hearts takes up all my time

Steamy Trails Publishing is more than honored to work with such a talent as Tiffany C. Lewis. She works tirelessly on her online magazine "Thematic Literary Magazine" the magazine was created to help new and amazing writers become professional authors. She states: We offer a friendly, competitive and helpful environment where writers can become professionals. For more information visit:
www.wearethematic.com

How has the "Steamy Trails" entity helped your literary goals?

"Steamy has enhanced my writing through great feedback and support. They have also brought me close to many other great authors. Before I was published I was able to get great insights from published authors."

~ Tiffany C. Lewis

TRINKETS AND BAUBLES
by Nike Binger Marshall

Corrine

I was quite content to live out the remainder of my days alone. Just me and my dog Lester. I had a few friends to keep life interesting, but for the most part, I spend and enjoy my time alone. My family lives in the next county, about two hours away. That's the way I like it. We may share the same DNA, but that's about all we seem to have in common.

My sister, brother and I all went to college and earned our degrees. My sister is a nurse, my brother is a surgeon, and I own a small gift shop right across form the Eaton Village bus depot. Yep...I sell stuff. My siblings seem to think selling trinkets and baubles is not important or life changing work. If the tangible impact on a person's life can't be calculated, the work is not worth doing. If that impact can't be calculated in dollars and cents, then it's the wrong business to get into. That is how they think. They are driven by material things.

"You're wasting you talent! Mom and Dad sent you to school for accounting and look at you! Working retail! You could do so much better, sis," my brother said at Thanksgiving dinner when I announced I was opening my own shop. My sister, in her attempt to be the peace maker said, *"Corrine, you could open your own accounting firm and eventually retire to the little gift shop,"* as if compromise on a dream was really an option. That was about 12 years ago. I haven't attended a family

gathering since. I visit my parents once a month, send birthday and Christmas cards to my brother and sister and their kids, and enjoy a peaceable life.

I went about the business of creating my own family. I met Ozzie in college. We married shortly before graduation, moved into a small house, got a mutt from the shelter and named him Lester. The ink was not completely dry on our degrees before we began trying to have children. We tried for five years and had three miscarriages. I endured 2 more years of in-vitro, and still did not have a child. My spirit was broken. I felt like a complete failure. What kind of woman couldn't carry a child to term? A damaged, incomplete, unfinished woman. That's what I told myself. I felt like God hated me. He had kept from me something so precious and important. Then to add insult to injury, He took my husband too. He died in his sleep on Christmas Eve. His heart just stopped. I stopped talking to God that day.

A few weeks after Ozzie died, I met Marissa Farmer. She arrived at the Winston Village bus terminal, which stands across the street from my shop, on a snowy Thursday afternoon. Her skin was over powdered with foundation that made her look ghost-like. She wore heavy black eyeliner, and her jet black hair was bone straight and just barely brushed her shoulders. She wore a black, leather jacket that seemed to have buckles and straps attached in random places, none of them fastened. Her denim skirt, also black, stopped about three inches above her knees. The gap between the end of her skirt and the top of her tightly laced combat boots revealed fishnet stockings. She carried a duffle bag, similar to the ones soldiers use. It looked quite full and if stood on end, it would have been just as tall as

Marissa. She got off of the bus, leaned her bag against the wall next to the bench outside of the terminal, and then sat down on the bench and waited.

I made myself busy around the shop, but as the day wore on, I noticed she was still sitting in the same spot. Something didn't seem right. I went out to ask her if she wanted to sit in the shop and wait for her ride. It was far too cold for anyone to sit outside in the snow

"Are you waiting for a ride?"

"No," she said.

"Oh! You must be waiting for another bus then?"

"No. I'm just trying to figure out what I need to do next."

"Why don't you come into the shop and warm up."

"Ok."

She grabbed her bag and trudged behind me back over to the shop.

I showed her to the upstairs bedroom and she left her jacket and bag there. I smiled when I saw a black and white spotted cow on the front of her black t-shirt. It was a little humor in her otherwise dark façade. I poured us each a cup of hot coco and we sat down on the leather arm chairs in the book corner.

She had a rough looking exterior, but she was very easy to talk to. She told me quite a bit about herself. She turned 17 a few days before her arrival to Eaton Village. She lost both of her parents the year before in a house fire. She was the only survivor. The police automatically thought she was somehow involved in starting the fire, mostly based on her appearance. She had no other living relatives that she was close to and felt comfortable living with, so she was sent to a foster home. She said her foster family wasn't horrible. They were very patient with her as she mourned her parents. She went to court and fought for the right to live on her own. The court granted her request and she decided to leave. She always wanted to live in Winston Village, so she packed her bag, bought a bus ticket and came to town. She had no other plan.

"There's just a lot of noise in my life right now, you know? I just need a quiet place to figure everything out. I don't know if this freedom is really what I want, but I think I'm doing the right thing," she said. Her voice was soft and husky. I had no reason to believe she was lying to me. I don't know what she said in particular, but something told me not to send her back to sit at the bus terminal.

"Why don't you stay with me while you try and figure it out?"

She looked surprised. But she offered a genuine smile and eagerly said, *"Yes! Thank you Miss Corrine."*

I knew she needed me, but I didn't know how much more I needed her.

Marissa

She came across the street like an angel. A fiery angel with long flowing dread locs that stopped at her hips. She glowed like a flame on a candle. She offered to let me come into her shop to warm up. When she realized that I didn't have a place to stay, she offered me a room in her apartment above the shop until I could find a place of my own.

The shop was as warm in appearance as Ms. Corrine. There was a counter filled with elaborate, handmade jewelry. There were fancy bottles and decorative vases and picture frames. On the other side of the shop was a sitting area. Well stocked bookshelves lined the walls. Chairs and ottomans were set up into groups in front of the bookshelves. Towards the back, Ms. Corrine had a dressing room and racks of shirts and dresses and scarves - all very exotic looking. In the middle of it all, was a dust mop looking dog she called Lester. He was gray and shaggy, not at all matching the golden warm of the shop or the owner...at least until he came over to check out the new person. He sniffed at my feet, made a sound that was something between a bark and a whisper and then put his paws on my leg and looked at me expectantly. I rubbed his head and behind his ears. He was satisfied. He shuffled back to his station in the center of the shop and plopped down with a grunt to resume his nap.

Ms. Corrine and I sat down on the far side of the shop along the wall lined with books. She brought a tray with tea and sandwiches. I told her a little bit about myself and the circumstances that brought me to Winston Village. She told me about losing her husband the month before.

"Ms. Corrine, I'm sorry to hear about your husband. I know you probably need space. I'll only be here a couple of days, top."

"No, no! You don't need to rush, really. I'd like to help you out. Besides, it will be nice to have someone around for a while. The last few weeks have been very lonely. The place won't feel so empty with another person around."

"What was he like? Your husband," I asked.

Ms. Corrine looked in my direction like she was a little uncomfortable with my question, but I could tell she was picturing him in her mind.

"He was quirky. He was like, a mad food scientist. He would combine the strangest foods. He fixed cranberries and pork chops one Thanksgiving. It wasn't too bad, actually. I might fix it for dinner one day, just for fun. He loved to eat bananas, spinach and mayonnaise on rye bread, with a dash of cinnamon and nutmeg. I tried it and hated it! I swear, he had an iron belly! There was one thing he used to do that I thought was weird. He tried to get me to do it, but it sounded so nasty! I couldn't wrap my mind or taste-buds around it."

"What did he do?"

She smiled, and let out a little chuckle, then said, "He bought this horrible tasting organic coffee. I think I still have some left in the cabinet. It tasted like bitter dirt. He would add honey and skim milk to it. He drank it all the time and swore it tasted heavenly," she let out a hearty laugh. She pulled herself together, but I noticed the tears on her cheeks. She turned away quickly and dabbed them with a hankie she kept in her sleeve.

"He sounded like a fun guy, Miss Corrine."

"He was. He really was."

"I know it's not easy talking about him. But that's how you keep him alive. Remembering helps to push the pain away."

She looked up at me. Her head was tilted to one side as she took in what I said. She continued to look at me and began to slowly nod her head. She picked up her cup and took a sip.

"Yeah," she said quietly, *"this is true. How did you get to be so wise for someone so young?"*

I blushed a little. "My parents used to call me an old soul. They said that when I was a baby, I was so serious. I didn't smile or laugh often. I would just look at people, like I was taking them all in and sizing them up. My mom said, grandma told her to take me to the doctor and have me checked. She thought I was deaf or had some sort of development issues. I just study people. I guess that's how I know things. I usually can see a person a mile off. I know if they are good or bad, just by looking at them."

"What did you think of me when you saw me," she asked.

"I said to myself, 'God sent me an angel.' I have no doubt He put me here for a reason."

Ms. Corrine looked me in the eyes but didn't say a word. She didn't look surprised. I think she sensed it too. I know she was having the same thought as me: What might God have in store for us for on this part of our journey?

Nike Binger Marshall, author of Persistence of Vision and winning selections in the Delaware Art Museum's I/Eye Witness Gordon Parks contest has made our hearts proud by sharing her noted talent for SteamT Pub's project. We thank her and urge you to visit her blog:

http://nikewrites.wordpress.com

How has the "Steamy Trails" entity helped your literary goals?

"It has been a source to promote my work, grow in my craft and encourage other like-minded writers."
~ Nike Binger Marshall

Beautifulosity
By Katrina Gurl

I get caught up when I look at you
Your stance, your posture and many possibilities,
The strength of your shoulders
Overwhelms me and keeps me grounded perfectly.

Your eyes are like windows
That allows me to peek into your cautious soul,
Your lips absorb my full attention
Each time zone you say good morning.

You stand firm within the essence of beauty
Your masculinity is perfect to capture,
It keeps me engaged
And Intrigued with only you.

You make love to my mind
Even when you think I have taken remission,
Your unsure confidence
Is your most appealing side.

I mask my excitement most of the time
When I hear you speak,
To hide the foolish little girl
That awaits your every word.

Yearning is nowhere near
Strong enough to make clear…
The private desires I have for you.
Your compassion and beautifulosity literally
overtakes me.

Contentment lines my soul
Each time you embrace me,
The pound of your heart
Always seems to match mine.

We continue to defy the laws
Of what unison really is.
We are connected the same way
A wave lines need to crash upon shores.

I feel you sensually
I welcome this farce daily,
The feeling of you shifts my soul
In between each 24 hours of you.

Accepting this reality
Is like simultaneous dreams coming true
With flashbacks of you.
And I wish to never awake from this.

A Real Lovers Ride
By Katrina Gurl

You have always given away the loverly things that were meant just for me. Passing it out freely like fiddle faddle being sold at carnivals and circuses. You justly say what was meant only for me as tickets for the next person in line and inclined to take your joy ride.

This rollercoaster is marked "A Real Lovers Ride".

You act as if I'm supposed to sift thoroughly through the used tags each day and come to some realization that this one or the other was the real tag meant for me. Just for me.

I am tired of you leaving my love on pedestals up so high that you forget to dust it off from time to time. I am tired of the ticket master forgetting his lines just before the show. Each ticket given has a show, right? Aren't you putting on a show?

Love is not an object or pawn to just be looked at or for the passersby's to say *"Awww look how pretty."* No, No, No! Love, is supposed to shine and BE shined upon, love is supposed to dance and BE danced with even if toes are stepped on from time to time.

My love has dance upon your toes on purpose. Not to heal hidden wombs, but because my heart, mind and souls was ready to not only dance, but take flight.

This love has spoiled me and the spoiled child within me never really wanted to share. This love has dressed me up as a true fashionista and I have never wanted to wear the same shoes that other girls wore. I want my stuff to be original and NOT copied. I never want to appear as if I were biting off of the next sista or competing for attention just to see who's arm looks better cuffed underneath yours.

This love can never be box office bought with smooth words that sooth souls or clever rhymes that make me sway a bit too it's potential.

My love is true, powerful and mind boggling. It is no way around my love, only through it. With a key that is. If destiny really means well, it would only come in by the use of a granted key. I remember handing you the key.

Only fools' buy tickets for shows they're already staring in. Only a fool see's love clearly and chooses to turn the other cheek.

Just to make sure this show is over, may I pinch your fat cheeks?

Creating and being part of this amazing project has been my biggest honor as of yet. To work with an array of such talented people for the cause of our youth overwhelms my heart with hope and inspiration for a better tomorrow. For more me visit: www.putawedgeinit.com

How has creating "Steamy Trails" changed your life?

The Steamy Trails organization has allowed me to clearly see the beauty and creativity that still resides in the world.
~ Katrina Gurl

WHAT'S YOUR WORTH
By Gloria Lathen

Each day you grace this earth
You should know your worth

You were created by the almighty
So that makes you royalty

Your value increases each passing year
You're worth so much my dear

You're a precious being
You're a part of the royal family you're a Queen
God has positioned his light on you so you can shine
Never entertain foolishness you don't have time
You're worth that and some
No matter where you're from

You're worthy of every blessing that comes your way
Queen I can only pray you know your worth on today

WHAT'S YOUR WORTH?

EVERYONE WON'T CELEBRATE
WITH YOU AND THAT'S O.K.
By Gloria Lathen

Some will be with you & some will not
You must keep pursuing your dream with all that
you've got

God has given you a gift that's all your own
Sometimes you will feel like you're alone

Do what you're called to do
And watch how God will reign down Blessings upon
you

When there's no one else
Clap for yourself

When folk have something to say
Never respond remain a calm it's going to be just o.k.

Folk is gone be who they are
You must be focused on setting the bar

Some folk will feel threatened by your success
Keep stepping you're blessed

What you should do
Is take a bow & celebrate you

EVERYONE WON'T CELEBRATE WITH YOU
AND THAT'S O.K.

STAND
By Gloria Lathen

I'll stand no matter what comes my way
Planted my feet will stay

I'll stand when folk speak ill of me
Smiling while moving towards my destiny

I'll stand when folk are not happy for me
I will praise my way through & give God the Glory

I'll stand when others come & try to discourage me
I'll just sit in silence & say watch you'll see

When I slip & fall
On that great name I'll call

I'll stand through the hurt & pain
Even in the storm & rain

I'll stand I'll stand and I'll stand
I fear no man

I'll stand & be who God created me to be
And that's none other than one classy lady

STAND

YOU DON'T KNOW WHEN TO CLAP
By Gloria Lathen

You sit there so quiet & still
And act as if God is not real

God has allowed you to see a brand new day
He keeps right on blessing you & making a way

This is the time to clap

He always arrives with your blessings on time
Ump, ump, ump he comes & just blows your mind

This is the time to clap

God forgives us for this & that sin
My, my, my guess what he'll do it again

This is the time to clap

You're wondering how you're going to pay that bill
Or what is going to be your next meal

God keeps coming through
And providing for you

This is the time to clap

YOU DON'T KNOW WHEN TO CLAP

I AM
By Gloria Lathen

I am more than what most think of me
I will remain the elegant woman I was born to be

I am a woman from head to toe
Yeah I just had to let you know

I am that diamond that's no longer in the rough
Hey now, watch out I'm working my stuff

I am the Queen God created me to be
It's not I but he that lives within in me

I am a loyal sistah indeed
Always present when there's a need

I am that woman they can't stop
There's no limit I stay reaching for the top

I am my Mother's & Father's DNA
I thank God for the woman I am today

I am the finish product you see before you
If you only knew what I've been through

I am my past & present all wrapped in one
I went from being in the storm but now I see the sun

IAM

Gloria Lathen uses her poetry to motivate, stimulate, and cultivate people to move beyond the ordinary and go for the extra-ordinary and she has done that and more to help make this anthology book a success. Visit her at:

www.glorialathen.org

How has the "Steamy Trails" entity helped your literary goals?

"It has helped me meet & network with many awesome Authors & Writers." ~ Gloria Lathen

My Confidant
By Emmanuel Brown

When times got rough
for me
tough
stuff
prevailed
you see
my mind-state wouldn't let me derail
SG

the best me
tried to surface,
my purpose
was found
to stop those trying to kick me when I'm down

My thinking was sound
I did my own kicking
bound
my own hands, I did my own sticking

Trying to be slick n'
really fighting with myself
fighting with my wealth
I was bad for my health

The damage done
in stealth
I hurt me for fun
years on the run
hiding from the son

The battle won
I lost face
and found grace

with peace of mental space
in a nice place

Life can't erase
scars and mental beatings
but meetings
with inner-self can lead to inner greetings

Leading
roles are ill fated
some are castrated
but each reading
is a scene that I created

I can't debate it
I dictated
my net worth
and I hated
many things that I regretted first

False images filled visions of grandeur
Waking up late
missing the worm then I slander

Anybody that stands still long enough
fighting for no reason
but to prove I'm strong enough

The season
was long enough
but it finally ended
mended
old wounds, found the right shade and blended

I befriended
comrades wanting what I want
finally finding the truth in my confidant

Special thanks to Emmanuel Brown, Founder and Chairman of Seeing Growth. He is also the publisher of I Am Royalty: Profiles in Black History anthologies, which are publications that serve as inspirational messages for young people. He can be found at
www.SeeingGrowth.com and
www.LabelMeRoyalty.com

How has the "Steamy Trails" entity helped your literary goals?

"Mutual support." -Emmanuel Brown

The Power in Forever
By Evangeline

Today I took a trip to the local library for the likes of him. Because every time I think of him, I immediately think of words like "powerful" and "forever". Now of course, we all know what those simple words mean. **Powerful** *means*: having or capable of exerting power, effective or potent according to the Merriam–Webster Dictionary and the findings made perfect sense, because that's just what he is; capable, effective and potent.

He takes over my mind and I am so eager to learn of him. He underestimates the true presents he brings to room. He commands attention, not because he seeks it, but simply because "powerful" never needs an introduction, it simply IS what it IS!

As I sat in the library, my mind began to wander a bit. Whenever I'm surrounded by this many intellectual thoughts on text, I tend to get a little overwhelmed by the knowledge that I see surrounding me.

I look carefully through each page to embrace its wisdom and then think to myself. *"What if the word "powerful" were to make itself human? I mean, a real human that could commune with us from in its purest form?"* Then I thought, *"Oh know, that wouldn't work at all, because if "powerful" were born as a human, it would be almost impossible to survive the fundamentals needed to get through a childhood."*

Children need to know that they are protected and sheltered. They need to know that their thoughts are cherished and words are counted for. Children need to know that they really matter. This prepares a child to face the world on their own terms, without the convictions of not feeling good enough.

Since "powerful" needs no introduction, who will cater to it? It sure looks strong enough to do for itself, right. Who will speak to it? "Powerful" speaks loud enough for the world to hear. Who will hug it?...for its stature is so grand. And lastly, who will acknowledge it?

The thought of "power" walking around in its own right kept my head in the clouds as I sat there in my local library. I proceeded to look up my second word "forever" and of course we all know what Forever means…it *means*: without ever ending; eternally, to last forever, continually; incessantly and always according to the Merriam–Webster that is.

Again, my mind is wandering and I thought to myself , *"What if "I" embodied forever and what if "I" became the "forever" that "powerful" needed to sustain itself?"* Maybe just maybe "powerful" could really form itself as human with "forever" on his side. Just imagining the "powerful" experiences a true follower like "forever" could teach the generations to come.

I must have sat there in that library thinking for hours. I was amazed with the duties I'd be taking on if this were at all possible. I immediately began reshaping my schedule so that "powerful" things always came first. I started taking notes on how I'd restructure the brokenness and loneliness he must of felt as a child growing up in not understanding his "power".

His "powerful" voice was so loud to others, but "forever" heard the whispers of his lost soul and there is so much he still needs to say. I quickly wanted to "forever" rush in and heal his wounds by listening to him, acknowledging his thoughts and cherishing them, letting him know that each one of his thoughts was now protected "forever".

I want him to know that "forever" will never grow old or tired of receiving the things that he has ever so carefully hidden away. "Forever" is a conscious decision to remain incessantly and she will always go completely out of her way to embrace his soul, so that powerful will remain forever.

Evangeline has trusted us with her first published work and we appreciate her efforts in making this book a success. Visit her at:
http://evangelinesecho2.wordpress.com

How has the "Steamy Trails" entity helped your literary goals?

"Steamy Trails has helped me acknowledge my try creativity and has pushed me to set action to it." ~ Evangeline Jalique

Esquires Maudlin [paradox]
By Kewayne Andre Clark-Wadley

The heavens erupt
as my lips have found salvation in
yours-
no earthly salvation
can compare
to the bliss found
in an angels care
my soul suffers for the sins
my body has yet to commit
I ask myself
is this the way to heaven
every twist every turn
more breathtaking than the next
everything I need can be found
in your grasp
everything I could ever want
everything I could ever imagine
meets the prayers
that have yet to be spoken
whether we dream together or in
silence
all I want is to be yours
all I'd ever yearn is to be yours
the hours that've turned into
days melt against the
chocolate laments
of our sealed hush waiting
as we've reached the horizon
our eyes have destined for..
before our words ever met
each other
before our imaginations ever
became each other's
the stars don't seem

as distant as they did before
merely gazing at the angels
as they frolic mongst
the different constellations that
long to become theirs
seeking the serenity
we both hope to find
in the hands
that have yet to become lost
in each other's
(the nights)
subdued to the silent cries
that's turned into the tears
baptized by (under) the moon that's
shone against your eye
mere butterflies that's turned
to the prayers that softly
lulls us to sleep
again I ask myself
is this the way to heaven

Before the Dawn [paradox]
Kewayne Andre Clark-Wadley

If I'm ever so fortunate to be blessed
with the longevity of your touch
I wish never to see the day
you leave this world before me
as I lay my head down to sleep
my only thought remains
take me before my eyes awake
let my hands cling on to hers tightly
let my last words be that I love you
more than my heart can bare
but take me before my heart breaks
to see the day you leave this world
before me
let my hand turn cold before
she realizes what happened
let her smile be the last thing that's
seen before my eyes close one
final time
but take me before she leaves this
world before me
let the warmth of her hand
cradle me once more
but take me before she wakes
and realizes I'm gone

Baptism [paradox]
Kewayne Andre Clark-Wadley

I can only hold you for so long
until light turns to dark
my eyes close and my head
lays against yours
postponing every possible second
that time would allow us to have
through my prayers you are
everything I could ever hope
through our reality my soul yearns
to become more than what my
fantasies would allow to be
presented as content
is it a crime that my lips wish to be
the only blemish that covers your face
is it a crime that my fantasies allow
me to caress you in ways your body
may tingle to feel
to please you in any way possible
to hold you for more than a nights
time
til you begin to see' that there's
nothing that can keep you away from me
as we disappear into the nights
horizon
Baptized against the winds
of each other's breath

The Caretakers Mistress [paradox]
Kewayne Andre Clark-Wadley

On this day I decided to write
to you once more
I miss the hands that use to sooth
me with every touch they decided to give
the days don't seem as bad
but the nights echo your voice
as the winds continue to whisper
through the old plywood
and the bright colored hues we both
picked out together
I use to hate this job
and the loneliness
that fills the coffins I watch nightly
but everything I didn't understand
now makes since
sometimes they talk to me
they reveal the pieces of my life that
I sorely took for granted
It's crazy how the simplicity
of something so simple can
mean the world
once the world you once knew ends
the only voice I long to hear is yours
this whole time I was chasing a
dream that in the end turned out
to be my own
I only wanted to provide the things
that I never had
that deep down I knew we both
dreamt of
but never once would I have thought
that I'd be the only one to watch the
sun rise on a dream that we both
built hand in hand

53

I miss you more than words can bear
I can still see your face whenever I close my eyes
my nights have gone sleepless
trying to forget but my Alzheimer's won't let me
On this day I decided to write
you once more
I miss the hands that use to sooth
me with every touch they decided to give
as I still stand and wait
not realizing that your heaven is
paved with streets of gold
and mine is paved only with the
intention of seeing you once more

Procrastination [paradox]
Kewayne Andre Clark-Wadley

I can never love you in procrastination
I can never fulfill my addiction without you
my stomach stands still
curious to where the butterflies have flown
curious to the thought
of what life would be like
without being by your side
don't let this life lead me towards the path
of that particular suicide
don't leave me alone
lost to the ways
of where I use to spend
my nights
woman I think to
share my last name
I can never love you in procrastination
I can never fulfill my addiction without you
my body aches for your touch
longing to become lost in you
as I hope you've become lost in me
my hands yearn to search you
in ways only dreamt
as all id ever want is to be the only
thing your eye lusts for
I can never love you in procrastination
I can never fulfill my addiction without you

How amazing to have the opportunity to work with such a talented young man. Kewayne Andre Clark-Wadley of Memphis, Tennessee, is a perfect example of what our youth's capabilities when encouraged to live their dreams. Learn more about him at: www.facebook.com/Romero.Amour

How has the "Steamy Trails" entity helped your literary goals?

"It has helped me to meet new people sharing the same passion in writing as me and also allows me to share my work with them." ~ Kewayne Wadley

ABC's of LOVE
By Damon Kimbrough

A- are u serious

B-bowing out gracefully

C-call it what you want.

D-didn't dial my heart

E-ended it before the start

F-find it funny it would be this way

G- gee I was a sucka

H-had u wide open

I-I was the one wide open, not you.

J-just shocked

K-kept me fooled

L-like a tool I was used

M-made it real evident

N-never again

O-out for dolo

P-pause

Q-quiet

R-retrace my steps

S-sucka for love

T-taught me a valuable lesson

U-under the influence

V-viciousness may be an end result

W-wow

X-x-ray needed, heart stopped.

Y-you play me like that?

Z-zen state of mind I must find

Diary
By Damon Kimbrough

I didn't judge you.
I kept your secret.
Never will I reveal it.
It's safe with me to keep it.

I didn't ignore you.
only adored you.
didn't make fun of you.
Just shook it off as nerves from you.

Stood up for you.
more than once.
but u chose your side
and now we're done.

I bid you farewell
I wish you nothing but the best.
but you will never know,
Intuition at its best.

So as I close this chapter
and turned the last page
this book has now ended
no more room left, you stole the last page.

Damon K. Kimbrough of Detroit was more than willing to help us in our efforts for this project. We thank him for sharing his talent, time and availability to make this project a success. Damon will be featured in future projects with SteamyT Pub, so stay tuned for more of his masterpieces.

How has the "Steamy Trails" entity helped your literary goals?

"By allowing me to express myself as a poet with liberty."

~ Damon Kimbrough

THERE HE IS!
Fiordaliza Charles

I WAS SEARCHING
HIGH AND LOW
FOR A MAN
ONE WHO WOULD
NOT FOLD AND MOLD
A MAN
WHO KNEW MY DREAMS
DID NOT LET ME GIVE UP HOPE
HE ENTERED
MY WORLD FELL IN THE RIGHT DIRECTION
DID I MENTION
I INSTANTLY KNEW
IT WAS HIM
THE MAN
I BEEN WAITING FOR
ALL THESE YEARS
WASTING TIME
LIVING IN FEAR
IT WAS YOU
THE ONE I'VE BEEN LONGIN FOR
NOW EVERYONE
REALLY WANTS TO KNOW
WHO HE IS
WELL LOOK NO FURTHER
THERE HE IS!

MY SOUL MATE
Fiordaliza Charles

I USED TO THINK
LOVE, WHAT IS LOVE?
I WAS NEVER THERE
IN LOVE
MY HEART WAS COLD
I DID NOT BELONG TO ANYONE
I THOUGHT THERE WAS NO ONE
AND THEN ONE DAY
I LOOK TO MY SIDE AND REALIZED
YOU'VE BEEN THERE THROUGH MY UPS AND
DOWNS
YOU'VE ALWAYS MADE ME SMILE
YOU'VE NEVER LET ME DOWN
YOU ALWAYS STUCK AROUND
I WAS SEARCH FOR LOVE NOT NEEDING TO
HERE I AM DEEP IN LOVE
WHO WOULD OF THOUGHT
YOUWOULD BE THE ONE
THE LORD KNOWS I'VE BEEN SEARCHING
NEVER THINKING IT WAS YOU
YOU ARE HERE BY MY SIDE
MY SOUL MATE
I AM SO HAPPY, I COULD CRY

YOU COMPLETE ME
Fiordaliza Charles

I FEEL THE FLAMES GROWING DEEP WITH IN

MY HEART
MY BODY
MY SOUL

I NEED YOU NOW AND FOREVER

TOUCH ME
HOLD ME
PLEASE ME

I LOVE YOU IN EVERY WAY AND FORM

YOUR EYES
YOUR HANDS
YOUR LIPS

I LOVE YOU FROM HEAD TO TOE

EVERYTHING THAT I AM
WHEN I AM WITH YOU
I KNOW I CAN DO ANYTHING
BECAUSE IT'S YOU
THAT COMPLETE ME

IT WAS YOU
Fiordaliza Charles

THE FIRST MAN THAT
TAUGHT ME HOW TO LOVE
IT
WAS
YOU
WHO SHOWED ME THE RIGHT PATH
AND HOW TO REMAIN STRONG
IT
WAS
YOU
WHO ALWAYS KNEW WHEN SOMETIIING WAS
WRONG
WHO SHOWED ME THAT LIFE GOES ON
IT
WAS
YOU
WHO TAUGHT ME HOW TO SMILE
EVEN THROUGH THE STORM
IT
WAS
YOU
WHO SHOWED ME TO BE PATIENT
AND TO BE A MOTIIER FIRST
IT
WAS
YOU
MY ANGEL IN DISGUISED
TO WHOM
 I COULD
NEVER SAY GOODBYE

THIS POEM IS DEDICATED TO MY
DAUGTHERS FATHER
ECLAYTON SMITH
R.I.P 7-8-79-7-15-11

NEVER SAY NEVER
Fiordaliza Charles

I'VE ALWAYS SAY NO NOT ME
BUT THE HEART DOES NOT LIE
IT KNOWS WHAT IT WANTS
YOU CAN'T TELL IT WHO TO LOVE

LOVE IS LOVE
YOU CA NOT CONTROL IT
BUT WHEN IT'S LOVE
YOU OWN IT

ALL YOU CAN DO
IS EMBRACE IT
TAKE IT
AND
TRY TO
MAKE IT

I USED TO SAY
NEVER, NO NOT ME
I WOULD NEVER
FALL IN LOVE

BUT LOVE HAS ITS OWN GOAL
WHEN YOU HAVE IT
IS LIKE A HIDDEN TREASURE
DID I FORGET TO MENTION
I WILL NEVER SAY NEVER

Fiordaliza Charles has been a writer since the very early age of 8 and has since then, shared her talent though many published books such as "My Poetic Heart". We are proud to have her veteran expertise within the pages of this book. To find our more about this amazing writer visit:
www.fiordalizacharles.yolasite.com

How has the "Steamy Trails" entity helped your literary goals?

"It gives me security as a writer, because Steamy Trails
provides a real Community and togetherness."

~ Fiordaliza Charles

Concrete Dreams
By Eddie Sharpe

Chains hanging down, they call it bling
Diamond studded ear stoppers, pinky Rings...
Trading in a future for their Concrete Dreams
Air Force Ones, a pair of top notch jeans
A shirt that is the epitome of fashion, and shades that
gleam...
Trading in goals for their Concrete Dreams
Tinted Windows, TV screens, leather seats stitched
with branded seams
24 inch chrome rims, with famous pop culture as the
color schemes...
They traded in livelihood for Concrete Dreams
Genuine smiles covered up with "precious" metals, or
so it seems
Hard eyes, mean mugs, with murder kill as the daily
themes...
Swapping out Authenticity for Concrete Dreams
Blurry eyes, empty bottles barely maintaining a lean
Blowing out soul after puffs of the blunt, acting
serene
Trading in health for Concrete dreams
Selling genocide to our people creating fiend after
fiend
Chasing the loot, bread, guap, dough, anything after
green...
Trading in responsibility for Concrete Dreams
Words used to describe our women is no less than
obscene
No matter how to justify what hoe, trick, or even
bitch means
Using them to gratify sexual needs as the daily
routines...
Trading in value of our queens for Concrete
Dreams...

Sending deadly messages to youth, and those in the
womb, unseen
Steadily wiping away the purity, leaving minds
unclean...
Trading in Generations for Concrete Dreams
No hard work, looking for beanstalks in magic beans
Misinterpreting the chase for wealth to obtaining it
by any means...
They traded in their Innocence for Concrete Dreams
Teardrops, Closed caskets, Mothers and Fathers
Screams...
They traded in their LIFE for Concrete Dreams

All I Know
By Eddie Sharpe

All I know is that she walks the earth as me...
She cherishes her birth as me...
And she doesn't view her worth as free...
But I do not know her identity...
But I know she is an entity...
All I know is that her soul is destined to intertwine
with mine, to become one divine being...
To become significantly more than what the
combined efforts of every single man has failed to
create...
To become words that mean more than great:
Marvelous, Wonderful, Amazing, Extravagant...
Exuberant...Incredible, Stupendous,
Phenomenal...Astonishing..
Remarkable, Sensational, Miraculous...
I have to say my longing for this undefined love is in
fatuous...
But let me stop...Because I do not know her...
All I know is that she has so much love that it emits
through her feet to the very earth that we both stand
on and I can feel her near me...
And her voice is faint...But one day I will hear her
clearly...
All I know is that she exists...She could possibly be a
part of my world now...
She could be someone that I gently grazed while
fulfilling the predefined steps that will lead me to
her...
And of course she may be someone I have never even
met...
Only because time doesn't feel now is a place for us
together yet...
All I know is that some man may be putting her heart
through games...

Making her jump through flames for love...
And see she jumps as high as possible...Because
that's how she loves...
But he's only an obstacle and I am at the end of the
course...
He was only the source of making her reach
capacity...
And with the force that she loves, I KNOW his heart
wouldn't have the audacity to survive...
All I know is that we are not searching for each other,
but will be one day...
We will cross paths and time will stand still as if it is
a priceless portrait forever capturing the moment that
our lives changed to become what no man can
fathom...
It shall then continue to create a lifetime full of bliss
and passion...
All I know is that I am making myself perfect so that
when I meet her perfection I will be fully aware...and
instead of her selection being full of despair, it will
be the best one she ever made...I long for her...And
that's All I Know.

I'm Going to Hang Her on My Heart
By Eddie Sharpe

Forever stained by the colors of past lovers, she fails
to realize that she is a work of art...
She looks in the mirror and swears she only sees
splatters of paint, but I can see the emotionally driven
strokes derived from her soul...
I can see the sad blues that humble her soul and give
her search purpose,
down to the resilient reds that helped her see the
danger of her anger...
And I can see the cautious yellows that hold her back
from embarking on her hatred...
My eyes can see the envious greens that have showed
her how to be selective in who she trusts her soul to...
Even the refined sophistication of violet that sparks
her desire to find love...
On a canvas that was surely the purest white once
upon a time...
But white canvases never reach the status of
priceless, only those that have been painted...In her
case tainted...
So her stains are actually immaculate expressions of
her inner desires...
For her past lovers are not the ones who placed the
paint upon the canvas, they were there to inspire...
and to simply provide the tools...Then they provided
the colors...

And with every love lost, she took those emotional
hues and expressed the pain all over her soul
eventually creating a passionate masterpiece...
And as men have searched far and wide for this piece
I believe I have discovered it...
Others have kept it locked away in basements, and
stashed up in attics...
Only making it worth more to the man who decides
to hang her on his heart...

Intensely
By Eddie Sharpe

I want her to love me intensely...
I want her propensity for love to be in the far right of
the bell curve,
and on a narrow road, to save love she'll swerve...
I want her love to be in the extreme degrees,
to the point that she burns to death for love...or is
willing to freeze.
I want her to love me intensely...
I want her love to cut my predefined dispositions of
relations so deep that it reinvents me,
creating a new individual who loves immensely...
Though it doesn't take much to convince me,
she said in her world things change
and that thing I been calling love is more like her
pain...
what days are sunny for me is what she calls rain
and my cleanliness is her stain...
See she has ascended to a level that I cannot attain...
To speak it in plain, the highest extension of my
emotional language is STILL lower than her
anguish...
Her love is so intense that to love she is a threat...
That's because nobody has reached this level yet...
And love is afraid that the embodiment of a human
can possibly take its place...See she scares love...
But not intentionally, it's just the nature of her
intensity...Her love just changes men accidentally...
She exposes them to something that they have never
known how to desire
and eventually their souls begin to elevate
higher...while on fire...
My soul will be waiting for her relentlessly until the
day I meet her intensity...

What Is Love?
By Eddie Sharpe

Love is that intangible thing that makes women
swing their hips, and makes men sing...
It is that untouchable expression of our desires that
ignites and inspires emotion...
Love is the indestructible force that acts as a barrage
of flames...
Engulfing the source of our hopes and exciting our
pains...
Bursting in the door of our hearts like full speed
monorail trains...
Leaving nothing but smoke in the path...
Leaving nothing but hopelessness, wrath...
Love is the undeserving blame for our emotional
afflictions...
Making our delusional preconceptions about love
matters of fiction...
Though the conviction we display when love arrives
is undeniably existent...
Love has no reasoning and is completely insistent...
But love is also that magical presence that persuades
us to do the impossible...
Gives us motivation to push the heart until
inoperable...

And in all honesty when love is at 100 percent that shit is unstoppable...
Love is the abstract manifestation of beauty and fascination...
Wondrous grace and ostentation...
The mediator of our found and lost relations...
Love is one of the reasons we give to show undying affection...
And when our soul suffers death, love offers the resurrection...
Love is the best infection...
Love reminds us that there is joy in the midst of misery...
Helps us understand how there is future in the middle of history...
Love offers an ever so gentle touch of mystery...
Love is the force that lives inside...
It protrudes from our presence blatantly, never hides...
Love is pure uncut truth, it never lies...
It gives our souls reason to live and without it we will surely die...

Eddie Sharpe, in our humble opinion is one of the most precise young writers we have had the pleasure of working with. SteamyT Pub is overjoyed and honored to have his writings documented for this project. To find out more about his writings visit his Facebook page here:
www.facebook.com/mrsharpeto

How has the "Steamy Trails" entity helped your literary goals?

"Steamy Trails has helped me learn skills that will follow me through my writing career. The range of help stems from constructive criticism, to unconditional support."
~ Eddie Sharpe

Let This Be the Day
By Robert Moore

Happiness

Beholds a longing spark
Initially, its gravitational pulls
Expanding the walls of my heart

A smile just for the brisk airs
A gleeful stroll in my steps
No sorrows to be dealt
No pain to be felt
That kind of happiness
A heart overflowing with joy
Even when I am by myself

The songs of my heart
Shall radiant
Definitive of cheer
To carry not a woeful soul
To expound upon my highs
When life gives so many lows

The type of happy
That makes me want to dance
And salsa the night away
A light that illuminates darkened spaces
Filling the void of empty places

To be of good cheer
My soul has long for many years
As I bellow these soulful tears
A joyful hymn is to reappear

A vigor in my steps
Pride in stride
Blessed be this day

As my joy radiates
My eternal suns reflected
As the Heavens open wide

Just Need to Know
By Robert Moore

Does she even love me?
I want to believe in her
If I could cut open my inside
Then maybe she could see
By all the degrees
As my blood flows
So does this idea of we
I just wonder
Does she even love me?

So many unknowns
Trying to piece it all together
For worse, for better
In her, I have found my forever
To be apart, I hope never

I wonder if she even thinks about me
If only she could see
The magnitude, these desires I hold
Deeper than intense cravings
Saving myself for she
Maybe the signals have crossed
Feeling as frequency is lost
The moment our paths crossed
I just knew something was there
I just knew we made the perfect pair
It's as if she came out of nowhere
With the intensity of whirlwind
My sphinx sitting upon my pyramids

When she not around
I feel as if my heart tumbling down
I do not want to listen to my heart
I do not want to rationalize

On this night, my souls ragging fit
As I plummet the pits of despair
Wondering if somewhere out there

Do

I
Even

Cross

Her
Mind

It just would be nice to know
So badly I want to let go
It's as if "now you see me, now you don't"
I want to give up on this notion
My devotion for she
This idea of We
But my heart just won't
Back and forth
Should I
Do I
Or I don't
Baptized her soulful redemptions
My condition arouses suspicion
Wondering…..
If this will be more of the same
Is this more of the same ole same

Understanding…..I try
One thing I know……How?

Because the heart never lye's……..

If only could know……

Somewhere

Anywhere

I just need to know before I take this leap of faith
I need confirmation; just don't want to make another
mistake

I just need to know……

I just need her to show me

Let me if we are to be…..

I just need to know…..

If this idea of we….

Will ever be…….

I just need her to tell me….

So that then….I can be free

Free to release my soul to thee…..
Can't stop thinking about her
Traces of her dwells within

But more than anything…….

This feeling I have…..A nagging surge

Purges penetrate my heart….Just don't want to make
a mistake

Just need reassurance that this occurrence of we

This idea of you and me……Is it fate……As I wait

My heart won't let me be…..I just need to know baby

I just need you……..Come……Just let me know

I just know it, I feel it my soul……You compliment the greater part of me…..

I just need to know……………..

Is There Such A Truth(Just For Me)
By Robert Moore

Thru your eyes.......

When you see me
You don't see my warmth
You don't see my pain
You don't see the many nights
These shattered ruins left dormant
Remains
Stains
Of a man with a broken heart
All you see
Is the outer shell of me
Not what dwells within me
You don't see
The many times
Left stranded
By the weaponry of mass deception
Since the day of my inception
No other than Gods hand of protection
You don't see.....
No matter how hard I try
Sticking to my code
An ode of one of the few good guys
You don't know....
I have had to sever many bad ties
Said my farewells
Still, simply doing what I felt was best at the time
Still, slandered to be this bad guy
All because I said my good byes
You couldn't let go
Wouldn't try.....Need closure
Asking me questions why....
But I tried.....thru and thru
All the jealousy

All the competition
Competing against another woman
I will admit….she's cute, she's fly
But for me, I am a man of character
And looks alone can't keep these eyes
I need to research a bit deeper
See what's inside of your heart
Hold a conversation
To understand the situation
To know
The when's
The what's
And the whys
And stop tripping on me
I am not the other guys
I am forthright
We all grown here
No need to tell any lies
Lust is deceitful to the naked eye
I have to pull back my retinas
From looking at your thighs
I am not that guy
Not holding space of pedigree
A timeless entity
Many befriend me
But when faced with challenges
How many will remember me
Still……
In your eyes
I'm just a sleeping enemy
Sending cards, candy, flowers
With the sweet scent of your perfumes
I have been the other man
I have shared many nights
In another's bed…….
But at the end, there is no kinship
Alone I hold my own in this friendship

My penmanship for the poetic song
Is the only air I breathe
Whether I am up or down
My flow always there when in need

Still......

When they look at me
All that I see is what the flesh wants
Not so much about what I need
I am nothing more than a quick fix
I am poetic therapist
Out of practice this very presence
When we converse
All they see is she, he
Or whomever
Nothing to do with me
Nobody cares about who I am
What I am passionate about
Or what ignites my flame
It's all about a late night thing
To kindle a spark
That has been long absent
For so many years
But I feel used up
Now, what am I to do?
Wither in tears
Maybe this is the reason
My heart harbors many fears
Lust.....That's all l see
Her seductive whispers
Piercing to my ears

What you see.....

Is a one-time thing
Orgasmic rhythms

You don't see me
You don't want my heart
You just like the idea
That I'm a good cook with damn good looks
But there is more to me, more than the cover of the book

So before you say you want to be with me

Would you take this man
In spite my many imperfections
Tell me…..Would I still be your numero uno
Would I still be your selection

Would you take me…..

If I didn't have a college degree
If I didn't feel like making love today
Would you…..Would you be okay with that

Would you take me……

All of me,

Not just the thing dangling between my legs
Would you take me not just for the flesh of me
Would you take time, to learn me, to understand me
To get to know the mind of me…..Because see
Everyone talks of mating, souls and chemistry
But me, myself…..I seek you to devour me
A deeper level of intimacy……Not just a one-time thing

I have had enough of all the superficial aspects
Doing all the right things, still getting no respect

And finally......

I was raised by a King and Queen
One thing that taught me
I want what they share
Immense chemistry
41 yrs. of marriage
Now that's what I call a winning team.....

Frankly........

I'm tired of love, not so much the phrase
But these modernized definitions
Connotations conflicted
A society that's lust addicted
Which leaves the lonely soul conflicted
Many images depicted....Sodomized by all this
fantasy

And yes....I am no prude
Not meaning to be rude
I too harbor sensuality
I too have my fantasy

But most importantly.......

I seek a deeper
Meaningful love

A love for me.....

A love for my mind

A love for my heart

A love for my spirit with in

A love that goes deeper than friends

A love that knows no ends

But see.......

All catch is all the residue

Just to get more of the same.......

But my questions I pose to God......

If you say you are of love........

Is there someone for me.....

Just me......Who can love me

Cherish me......Embrace me

The way that you do.......

Make a believer......Make this my truth

So that I can be free to say those three words............

I LOVE YOU

AND

I DO......

Make me a believer

Make me a receiver

I just need to know

Is there such a thing….

For me…..Will this ever be true……

Hoping He Hears Me
By Robert Moore

An unsettling purge
Moves thru my spirit
Incoherent to His calls
My mind is cluttered
Cast asunder the rubbles
I must take heed
So much I need
In the midnight hour
I plead
Calling out His name
Hoping He hears
I hearken to His call
These piercing darts of iniquity
An onslaught is fought
Sin raging within
I open my mouth to speak
I have fallen weak
I don't even know where to begin
Feeling as if I am at wits end
I can't pretend
The enemy devours
Every fiber of my soul
So on this night
As my quail scrolls
These naked pages
Purging rages all senses
So many times
I thought it was fate
Many times
By my own will
I made many mistakes
Please take this load
To much a burden to carry
I tarry not to fear

Right now
My Sheppard
As I plead
It is YOU
Your voice
I desire to hear
My souls weary
My eyes teary
I dispose of man-made theory
I close my eyes
The still of silence
Just so I can here HE
Hoping He responds to me
I need direction
I need to stay the course
Fighting these darkened forces of fear
It's YOUR voice
The only voice I want to hear
Trying to rationalize
Trying to make things clear
I pour out all of my soul to thee
Why is it
I feel as if you have forsaken me
So many hate me
So many come against me
A senseless scheme
My mind deviates
Trying to remain straight
Feeling as if my time has passed me
I need your divine hands to orchestrate
Motivation has left the seem
At one time, I had a dream
To be all you made me to be
Tussling these demonic forces
I just want to be set free……..

I call unto you tonight

I hope you hear me
I can't do this alone
But
Tonight
My plight
That stands before me

Feeling destitute

Feeling forsaken

Maybe I'm mistaken

Still…..

I know in my heart
You didn't leave me here

To do this all on my own…..

But right now….

Afraid and alone

I just need to know

Because I can't do this on my own……

Can I Have This Dance
By Robert Moore

Would I be wrong
To share these many inhibitions
Positioning my heart to display
To show you in so many ways
My inner longings of heart
Thoughts of you continue tugging away
Awaiting the day, when I can come your way
Writing my essay across your heart
A connection of souls
Two minds become one heart
As our flesh suppressed
An intense want
Our eyes meet
Anticipation begs of your smile
Explorer your canvas
An outpouring sours
Dampen me your reservoirs
To touch your skin
A change descends
Saturate me your love
Drench these aching pores
To hold you close to me
As our mouths part
My precious mahogany
Inseminate me your inscriptions
This fixation for you
Plunges my loins
As my hand gently
Expands
To caress every inch of your canvas
Drench me your ripened nectar
Many thoughts I reflect
Dissect me your warmth
Let's dance away

A wide array of abstracts
Embody me your secretions
Inflict upon me your many inhibitions

Let's do our own salsa
Moving the rhythms
The drum roll of this lover fete
I just want to touch you
Taste you
Feel the thump of your every heartbeat

Two minds
Two hearts
Two souls

Become one

Know that you make me complete
From the follicles of my hairs
To the very souls of my feet
As we dance the night away
As we groove the rhythms………

Of this lovers drumbeat……….

Robert Moore, is the self-published Poet/Author of
"The Love Jones Diaries." His writing is parallel to
greatness and we appreciate his talent and creativity
in helping with this project. Visit him at:
www.styleszone77.blogspot.com

How has the "Steamy Trails" entity helped your literary
goals?

"Inspirational, helpful and dedicated is what Steamy Trails
is to me." ~ Robert Moore

The Recovery (One Man's Sin)
By Martin Pounds

My mind is racing no sign of tracing,
my life in this unholy land, wondering
what's the plan can't understand the
recovery of this man's plan. Set in stone his
commandments are whole everyday
Can I turn this around pick my faith of the ground,
memories are sound with the Angels of heavens
coming down,
time past I need to the recovery of my life must last.
As I walk thru valley of the shadow of death with one
tear
that I have left.

Can one man's sin be his downfall within or free fall
from all.
 He cries out to the Lord save his soul trap between
the walls
that has despise him from all. Let the truth be told,
unsaved
A life seems worthless with doubt and shame as evil
calls his name but the Angels call may the truth be
told
it was written from old. From the depths of his soul
let his
story to be told as the recovery unfolds. Now this is
the day
 as he reclaim his faith the erase the agony and pain
who may
 understand the journey he made his life mirrors the
image
 that his dreams had laid. Soul no one left to hold
future is less bold.

The Rebirth
By Martin Pounds

It's comes to this
decision that I put myself
in this prison I'm spinning
out of control the other side
of life has me in a choke hold.
Some say that I'm too old but
this is where wisdom unfolds.

I been thru the pain and I cause
some along the way as I stare
myself in the face there's a
side of me that I really hate.
Now this where my rebirth takes
place to prepare for my return in
a new way.

I feel that my life was put on
pause and in return I almost
lost it all and from the goodness
of my heart I have to make a
fresh start. What is the price
selfishness yes there is a difference
that had me walking a little different.

Almost broke the trust of my friends
now do I really deserve them time
to realize there's over the hill and
thru the skies. I drop down on my
knees pray holds the key to my release
of this bad energy that speaks. There
no repeat I feel so free and finally found
some peace.

My soul is cleansed and stress free
now I can stand on my own two
feet. Some think I will fail and
become weak but little do they
know what's the driving force inside
me. Born to be nothing less my first
and middle name says I'm the best the
rebirth of me is the test while some
suffer from manic depress.

Change the World
By Martin Pounds

We are in need of change

there's so much pollution on the

brain. Father can you hear us our

world has fallen down you're the

only one that can hear our prayers

now. Out of the darkest into the light

may our souls gives us strength in this

world that has fallen by mankind.

Only to make it right stand hand to hand

 as we look to the sky.

Whispers in the dark that link us to

the past the threat of global warming

rise waters with storms and elements

seems to clash. To correct each

problem is a tall task with starvation

killing the next generation and we

worrying about racist and without enough

vaccines to past how long will the sick last

from these plagues you ask.

Can you hear the victory our soldiers
marching with every beat it's been to
long road to watch the world come undone.
Still we not finish we have to stand firm
and in position. World domination that for
thought we can't let history repeat. We need
peace when it was good just like the beginning
of time. A miracle is on the rise with rains
showers us out of heavens skies.

Long Ago
By Martin Pounds

It's been so long since
I found your hearts mend
feelings end a distance journey
without a friend. The pureness
soul searches where the innocence's
of love is kept. No more time to lose this
woman bare wings that heaven has sent
that I cannot refuse.

As days turn into nights longing for
your touch as clouds set in the blue
skies and rivers turn into waterfalls
it's your love I have waited for cry me
a river no more this path that use to be
a long road has given me great distance
in what I seek. The presence of you my
sweet fills like the moon over the sea.

Loneliness is not a best kept friend
it's the end of the road that's where
it ends. I fought so hard and now this
meaning is the beginning waves crush

against the ocean shore the twinkle in
your eye from so long ago each day
like opening another door forever more
it's you by my side like the sun sets at
night. And if we were meant to be wind
that whispers like chimes now time has
a new dawn with love that kept us away
so long. Now together with our future
alive just like it was from the beginning
of time.

Freedom of Love
By Martin Pounds

See sometimes I need to find
that love that is so special and
essential that will set me free. A
woman that would play for keeps
that immaculate force of what I
need understanding the true nature
that is deep in me. Loves rapture of
the freedom that I'm after a gentle
kiss that sparks a movement like this
to get you to groove like this and when
you walk into a room all I can say is hey
you dim the lights with every shade and
the scent of your perfume I can trance you
and my heart is open what's your next move.

Every moment in time there's a twinkle in
your eye you know this is our season two
lovers rekindle just like a shooting star flickers
across the sky it gives us something to believe
in. I was lost out to sea you gave me a lifetime
I can't catch my breath because I have so much

to say I can't wait another minute or a single

day and with chance you I can hear the bells

that ring it's freedom of love that blooms.

A special thanks to Author, Poet and Artist Martin Pounds for sharing inspiration and creativity to make this project special. To learn more visit: www.facebook.com/thewriterspoet

How has the "Steamy Trails" entity helped your literary goals?

"Steamy Trails is home to me. A place to freely flow my talent." ~ Martin Pounds

Sista
By G. D. Grace

Sista, don't you know

That behind that banging body you're so much more?

You're a daughter or a mother and child of God

Not just curves and breasts that spill out your bra

You've got fire and sass within your soul

Such grace and rhythm in that urban stroll

Afrocentric in an array of colors

Not just some arm piece for an egotistic brotha

Start opening your mind instead of your legs

Stop giving in just because he begs

Listen to your heart and hear your voice

To make that move towards the better choice

For only you can become change

And take the path to that higher plain

To be a woman whose in tune with self

Instead of a body and nothing else

There more to you than what catches his eye

And it's time to prove it and defuse the lie

Sliding down that pole just might pay a bill

But tell me sista, how do you really feel?

To be an object rather than a prize

By selling off what's between your thighs

Listen here and listen close

What is it that you love the most?

Is it cash to buy that diamond ring?

Or your self-respect, that other thing?

I'm telling you there's more to life

But it's up to you to see the light

Sista, don't you know…

Here I Stand
G. D. Grace

Let me explain something to you…

You see these scratches on my knees are only
temporary…

and the dirt on my face from having fallen down can
be washed away,

but one thing still intact is my spirit…

You see, it belongs to a power that I cannot even
fathom…

It is resilient

It is strong

It takes a licking and keeps on ticking…

It was designed to get me through this thing called
life…

As a human being my body has limitations, however,
my soul is vast…

Because it was born out of a love more powerful than
anything I can see…

When people hurt me I recover…

When my purpose is interrupted I always find my
way…

Somehow
Someway

I rise upward from the ashes of mourning and
disappointment...

temporary discouragement might rattle the cage on
the outside

violent bouts of frustration will sometimes barrel
down on my mental,

yet I emerge like the light of another day...

out of the darkness...

renewed

stronger

wiser

my feet are planted on sacred ground...

my eyes are always fixated upward towards the
heavens...

inside of me I am warmed by a divine spirit...

I've been knocked down repeatedly but I'll always
get back up...

Here I stand...

What else have you got?

I'm not going to stay down for long...

Here I stand…

Here I stand…

Sweet Relief
by G. D. Grace

It seems there are moments in life that challenge existence, disturbing situations and encounters that shred the spirit like eight by ten, eleven inch paper, destroying emotions with little regard for the collective labor involved producing the effort. During those agonizing moments, everything appears to have been ripped apart from the heart, like raw meat being pulled away from the bones of lifeless prey. Every thought has been contaminated with painful memories that cannot be erased, and the overwhelming feeling of loss overpowers practical senses and all you can see is the before, the during, and the after repeatedly.

Breathing becomes a task requiring focus and will, and it's done out of necessity as opposed to desire, because the purpose of your very existence is lying in the gutter, badly bruised and deeply troubled. You begin to wonder why sunshine feels cold, why rain drops seem to burn the skin, and why every limb on your body has gone numb, but there are no answers to explain the emotional distress that has enslaved the spirit.

The emptiness echoes throughout your inner cavity ferociously, drowning out time and space, paralyzing all senses, leaving you defenseless against the violent war raging within. There's an unrelenting ache shooting throughout every bone of the ivory structure holding you together, and you struggle to hold every piece together, praying that at some point you'll hear a lone horn in the distance announcing the arrival of relief, and that is the only possibility keeping your mental balance from succumbing under the weight of the hurt.

You begin to treat tomorrow as if will never come, like it is an enemy because you feel as though all it will bring is more anguish, disappointment, and uncertainty. You hurl stones at hope during an exasperated tirade, trying to ward off its efforts to save you from slipping further away from reality, but find that you cannot stop it from reaching out to you.

Consumed in darkness, you hold tightly onto the window blinds trying to keep the light from billowing in, fearful of facing another day and too frightened to

move ahead.   Just when you think you have foiled
faith's efforts, it reaches in and pulls you out,
wrapping it's arms around you.

Finally...

Finally...

Sweet relief.

In our professional opinion, G. D. Grace is one of the most brilliant literary minds of our time. His work ethics and creativity has become a standard for us to visually see what it looks like to travel a journey of success. We are honored to have a portion of his accolades in this book. Find out more of his writings by visiting:
http://author2be.wordpress.com.

How has the "Steamy Trails" entity helped your literary goals?

*"The **comradery** is endearing."*

The Lamp Post
By Michael Charles Givens

If only that lamp post could talk,
oh, what stories it would tell.
It would tell tales of those who walk
on this street it knows so well
...
All the people come and people go
Homes are build and they fall
But the lamp post is in the know
Because it's been there thru it all

It would tell of the little girl at play
with her little friends near the street
But in her home her parents pray
Because there's not enough food to eat.

The lamp post saw the woman that cried
Exactly Three years ago tomorrow
Her only son was shot and died
Now her life is filled with sorrow

It would tell you of the young man so proud
to go to school with his books on his back
But he grew up and ran with the wrong crowd
and now he's strung out on crack

The lamp post has been there seen it all
on this street that he has stood
The lamp post knows as it stands tall
It'll get better if we work for the good

~ Em See Gee

You'll Never Sleep Alone
By Michael Charles Givens

I wanted
you appeared
I pursued
you relented
I persisted
you succumbed
I yearned
you provided
I embraced
you melted
I loved
you trembled
Nothing has ever
felt quite as natural
as you in my arms.
The sensations pulsating
in my loins
communicates to my mind
that love has arrived with
a vengeance.
Heaving thigh sweats.
Lovely vibrating flesh.
Gyrating bogy parts.
That smile of supreme
satisfaction on your face
as you drift off to sleep.
I stare at your beautiful face
engaging every bit of restraint
in my being to keep from
waking you.
You have touched me.
You have aroused me.
I have loved you.
Now you lay there

asleep with that look on your face
That look like all your wildest dreams
have come true.
Mine have.
I love you.

~ Em See Gee

Street Memorials
By Michael Charles Givens

Bar on all windows, locks on all doors.
Drunks on every corner, thugs and crack whores
Safely in my car trippin the ghetto route
By a fence I saw lit candles, I knew without a doubt
that a life had been taken, blood had spilled there
needlessly forsaken, pain too much to bear
Spirits of the dead silenced heart beats
Street Memorials and mourners populate the streets
I made a left A Street, on Main I made a right
Near a fence I saw the remnants of another gun fight
Candles, flowers and pictures near a front yard
Living in this Ghetto sure is gettin hard
What can we do? What can we say
For this senseless violence to simply go away
Left on C Street, a right on Chang
A right on D there I heard a "BANG"
Blood leavin bodies, cadavers on the ground
I pray for his soul, I am homeward bound.

May God bless everything you touch

~ Em See Gee

Michael Charles Givens, our brother, gifted writer and longtime networking friend has shown us that there are no limits to his writing ability. We are happy to share his masterpieces in our first edition of SteamyT Pub anthology books. Michael helps to make us look good! Visit him at: www.thedopelesshopefiend.com

How has the "Steamy Trails" entity helped your literary goals?

"Because of Steamy Trails, I now write poetry and short stories prolifically and am on the precipice of publishing my second book." ~ Michael Givens

Invincible
By WiL Palazzo

Say goodbye to arguments and petty lies
Losing love and worthless tries
And laying in a bed for one that's really made for two
Harsh goodbyes and worse hellos
Saving lives and taking blows
No more taking bullet holes; I'll take them all for you.

Your love could shatter any gun
I'll hold my ground, no way I'd run
Either this is real or just really convincible
And at the end of the day
There's nothing anyone could say
They can't bring me down; with you, I'm invincible.

In the dark you are my light
Guiding me throughout the fight
I almost lost my hope and trust in a memory
I'm impressed, you look right through

Every corrupted thing I do
Now all my hope and trust is that you'll see...

With you I'm invincible

Untitled
By WiL Palazzo

A crystal future
Reflected in fire
Ensconced in brilliance
Unbearably hot
A furnace of light and thought and sound

Innumerable glittering possibilities
Countless roads we might travel
Individuality a heavy cross to bear
Knowing how high the flame can grow
But almost afraid to stock the fire
So many things left unseen and in shadow
Horrendously vast eternity
Weeps with fear
Of what will be wrought
In the weighty transient moments
That compose our lives

A gunshot in the night
Born of fire and passion and violence
We hurtle through this world
Through the darkness we twirl
A deadly dance of life and death
Until finally we fall
Spent we tumble to the ground
And so in this fleeting existence
An eye blink in life of Time
We must remember to hold certain things dear
Certain things should never be taken for granted

And there are those select few
Chosen brilliant flares of light
Exploding amongst the countless dim sparks
Worshipped, cursed, envied

The flames that burn brighter
Whose after image lingers longer
Drifting before out twirling eyes
Caught up in the dance of time

And every once in a long while
The liquid eye of being opens
Our souls look up and see
What we thought we knew
Threatens to be blown away
Cast into the fires of reality
The furnace of change opened wide

But what of those dimmer sparks
And their twinkling ballads?
Played out upon this stage
Hidden from the public's unblinking eye
Whispering their dramas in brittle silence

Have they any less value or worth
Because their flames are not as bright?
They still pass through this world
Souls cast in iron or glass, each a work of art
Do they contain less magnificence
Simply because they are not on display?
Museums cannot contain all the art of the world
And what are the people we walk amongst other than
breathing sculptures?

We don't always have to look to the brightest stars
Even the dimmest of these celestial candles can bring
out our hearts
Let our eyes wander elsewhere to find light
For there is artistry in even the darkest soul
And let us celebrate the whispers and shadows
Hidden dramas and unnoticed dreams
Let us embrace dim stars and dying flames

Adding their light to our own and brightening the
entire sky
Instead of a few distant points of light

The human life is a thing of inconceivable value
A strange mixture of rain and sunshine
Makes up the liquid eye of being
The souls that dwell within us more precious than
any gem
And each is utterly unique hand crafted work of art
A living painting that breaths and moves
All together making up the portrait of our world

And whether or not I am meant to shine brightly or
dimly
I will never forget that no matter how much someone
shines in this world
There are countless lives, points of light all around in
the night sky
And none is more valuable than another
For they are all priceless

Frozen
By WiL Palazzo

I wish this was easier, or I was stronger
But a wish is just exaggerated hope
And I've cried my reserves dry
So maybe that's why I'm here
Sitting at this table for two
Wishing you were sitting across from me
 Ready to piece together my heart
One fragment at a time

The truth is, it hurts constantly finding out
Your puzzle pieces just don't match
I wish I could stop feeling like I'm broken
Slowly I'm learning to suppress my emotions

Cold winter nights help my progression
As the snow covers me and my faults
The pain is buried in a numbing white blanket
And for once, I begin to feel at peace

As I drift out of consciousness
Dreaming of happier memories

The morning sun; another day
And so melts my protective sheet
It's now when all the pain comes rushing back, I say

"I'm sorry…I don't want to hurt you anymore"

 But I'm not strong enough to change

So maybe, one of these days
When the sun comes up
And the last of my mistakes rinse over my body
I'll be forgiven, and I'll have left in peace

WiL D. Palazzo provokes passion, imagination and remnants of an aged writer beyond his years. We are honored that he is a part of this project . Visit the link below to enjoy more of his unique style of writing. www.steamytrails.com/WiL_D.html

How has the "Steamy Trails" entity helped your literary goals?

"It provides a genuine place filled with support for people aspiring to be writers" ~ WiL Palazzo

Be a Part of Something Bigger Than Yourself

100% of all proceeds of this SteamyT Pub Anthology Book goes towards our *"Young Writers Flow Project"*.

To become a sponsor or if you are a youth interested in benefiting from this project please contact visit the Steamy Trails Publishing website @ www.steamytrailspublishing.com or contact:

Katrina Gurl
Steamy Trails Publishing (Stockton)
PMB 708 1163 March Lane Ste. D.
Stockton, California 95210

Nita Bee
Steamy Trails Publishing (Detroit)
P.O Box 28459
Detroit, MI 48228

For This Cause Writers Unite

Thank You For Your Support!